What people are saying about Singing Lessons for Little Singers:

I am a piano/voice teacher who has been asked to teach younger children than I am used to. I am so thankful for this book which helps guide me to the special needs of children and what they can absorb at that age! It is a wonderful age-appropriate book and I hope there will be more to follow!

Helen J. Hutchison (Amazon.com)

As I read through your 'new singing method book,' I was aware that you have accomplished something that has been needed for a long time. A method book for young voices has been needed for many years, and you are to be commended for filling this void. It is true that little has been done to really teach children the proper way to sing, although we have many children's choirs that do very well collectively. Individually, they still lack the proper knowledge of how to sing correctly. Your method book is a pioneer in this field.

Doyle West (Public School Music Teacher, Administrator and Clinician)

This curriculum has literally revolutionized the vocal department of our performing arts studio! Where has this book been for the last hundred years???! I have searched far and wide for the perfect private lesson book and now I have found it. Please, please, please come out with Book Two as soon as possible!

Lissa Morris (Director of Allegro Performing Arts Studio, Edmond, OK)

We want to know what you think! Send us your comments and experiences about *Singing Lessons for Little Singers* and you may find them on this page in a future printing. Send your comments by email to **questions@littlesingers.info**.

Visit us online at **LittleSingers.info**
or on **Facebook (keyword "Singing Lessons for Little Singers")**

Singing Lessons for Little Singers

A 3-in-1 Voice, Ear-Training and Sight-Singing Method for Young Children

By Gregory Blankenbehler, MA

Illustrations by Erica Blankenbehler, DC

Pitch Perfect Publishing Company

Singing Lessons for Little Singers

A 3-in-1 Voice, Ear-Training and Sight-Singing Method for Young Children

By Gregory Blankenbehler

Illustrations by Erica Blankenbehler

Additional cover formatting by Allen Wilson

Printed in the United States of America

Published by the Pitch Perfect Publishing Company
http://pitchperfectmusic.org
questions@pitchperfectmusic.org

Introduction

The incredible benefits of early music education on intelligence and success in life have been long known and shown by such universal geniuses as Leonardo da Vinci, Isaac Newton, Albert Einstein and Stephen Hawking. Recent studies have concurred that early music training can produce greater physical development in the brain,[1] and up to 27% higher math,[2] 57 points higher SAT[3] and 46% higher IQ scores.[4] Approximately 22% more applying music majors are admitted to medical schools than any other major[5] and "the very best engineers and technical designers in the Silicon Valley industry are, nearly without exception, practicing musicians."[6]

Singing Lessons for Little Singers was designed to fill the current void of materials for private teachers of very young voice students. This revolutionary method provides age-appropriate voice training using proven pedagogical principles and healthy vocal technique for children between the ages of about 5 and 9. Combining a system of voice-developing exercises, a progressive ear-training and sight-singing course and a repertoire of fun and exciting songs with entertaining lyrics and delightful illustrations, this powerful method has had great success in teaching children advanced singing skills and instilling in them the enjoyment and desire to continue in their musical studies and become exceptional individuals.

To the Teacher

Singing Fundamentals: The first unit of *Singing Lessons for Little Singers* is a basic introduction for the first-time student to singing lessons. The stretches, posture, breathing and register exercises are designed to be done at the beginning of every lesson before moving on to more current exercises. Regular repetition of this routine will help the little singer mentally and physically "get in the zone" for each lesson, as well as reinforce proper fundamental techniques.

Each of the subsequent units is organized around a fundamental measure of musical pitch, from a basic introduction of the scale through each interval, up to half-steps and the minor scale. (Research has shown that by introducing each pitch interval individually from the smallest up, young children are able to more successfully build their pitch accuracy and tonal quality.)

Exercises: Each unit begins with one or more exercises to help the little singer become familiar with the interval being taught. These exercises should be modeled vocally by the teacher (always in the register indicated, not an octave lower!) and then accompanied for the student on the piano, transposed up and down by half-step as far as possible. Again, regular repetition of these exercises will ensure the student's success in learning to sing well. While exercises can of course be phased out as the student progresses, certain ones should periodically be reviewed and others should become part of the student's regular warm-up.

Songs: The songs in *Singing Lessons for Little Singers* are also grouped according to the interval being presented, as well as difficulty. Once the little singer has mastered the interval exercises at the beginning of the unit, he or she is ready to start learning the songs. It is suggested that these songs be approached as a fun activity to be learned and then frequently revisited as a game might be. In this way, the student will learn to think of singing and lessons as a pleasurable activity, rather than a chore. Songs should initially be learned in the most comfortable key for the student and then transposed to work the different parts of his or her voice. At first they should be accompanied only by the melody, and then later with only simple chordal accompaniment. As the student progresses in skill, the accompaniments should become more complex and the melodies phased out to develop the little singer's vocal independence. Additional songs appropriate to the student's progress are suggested in the introductory statements of each unit.

Technique: At the end of each unit is a technique section designed to work on the little singer's tone, diction, flow and performing skills. These sections do not address musical intervals and can be used independent of the rest of the unit. Since the concepts and skill they present are often difficult to completely master, they should be reviewed frequently but with special care to not frustrate the student.

Supplementary Materials: In addition to *Singing Lessons for Little Singers*, it is suggested that the advancing student begin using additional songbooks; perhaps a second book of favorite folk songs and a third of Disney songs as the student advances in skill sufficient to sing them. The following are some suggestions:

> *The New Illustrated Treasury of Disney Songs.* Hal Leonard, ISBN 793593654, $29.95
> *Disney's Princess Collection – Complete.* Hal Leonard, ISBN 634033875, $17.95
> *The Big Book of Children's Songs.* Hal Leonard, ISBN 0881889423, $14.95
> *The Best Children's Songs Ever.* Hal Leonard, ISBN 0793589665, $19.95
> *The Reader's Digest Merry Christmas Songbook.* Reader's Digest, ISBN 0895771055, $29.95
> *The Best Christmas Songs Ever.* 5th Edition. Hal Leonard, ISBN 0881889288, $19.95
> *Get America Singing...Again!* Vol. 1. Hal Leonard, ISBN 0793566355, $16.95
> *Get America Singing...Again!* Vol. 2. Hal Leonard, ISBN 0634015486, $19.95

Additional Suggestions: The best pedagogical methods for little children stress logical structure, repetition, review, visual and auditory demonstration, and short-term goals and rewards. *Singing Lessons for Little Singers* uses all of these principles to most effectively teach its students comprehensive musicianship, as well as quality singing. In order to best take advantage of this method, it is suggested that the teacher do the following:

- Praise the student after every exercise and song, and reward the mastery of a unit or song with a sticker.
- Regularly review previous exercises and songs, approaching them as returning to a fun game or accomplishment in which the student has already proven their skills. Balance review with learning new material to keep the student from being frustrated with either.
- Refer to the illustrations and musical notation in the book when explaining concepts or teaching songs or exercises. Teach and practice reading notes with the student when learning songs and exercises.
- Always model songs and exercises in the same register (octave) as the student sings it. (This means that a male teacher will often be singing in falsetto.)
- Work on all parts of the voice—both low and high—by regularly transposing songs and exercises up into the student's head voice. While progress may be slow, regular use will help the student's comfort and development in the high voice.

To the Parents

I commend you for choosing to bring music into your little son or daughter's life. While these lessons have the potential to begin a wonderful life-long talent in your child that will bring great satisfaction, they will more importantly bring him or her greater confidence, intelligence, learning and studying skills, and performance and presentation ability. Perhaps the foremost expert on child music training, Shinichi Suzuki said: "The purpose of [music] education is to train children, not to be professional musicians but to be fine musicians and to show high ability in any other field they enter.[...]There is no telling to what heights children can attain if we educate them properly right after birth."[7]

As always, you as the parent will play a crucial role in your child's music education. While the teacher will act as the "musical guide" teaching concepts, exercises and songs in lessons, you will be responsible for much of your child's retention and progress between lessons. This is easiest and best done by becoming your child's "practice partner." Observe the exercises and songs taught in the lessons and then lead your child in one or more short practice sessions each day. While your child can still progress without practicing, your efforts will cause their talent to multiply. When your child has reached sufficient maturity, you will find that your physical presence will be less and less needed in practice and lessons.

Whatever level of involvement you choose to take, it is of the utmost importance that you always remain positive and supportive of your child's musical interest and progress. Frequently encourage them to perform for you what they have learned and reward them with much affection. As a parent, being your child's greatest fan will not only ensure their interest and dedication, but also help build a wonderful and precious relationship between you and them. I wish you the best of success in raising your exceptional child!

—Gregory Blankenbehler

About the Author

Born into a family of musicians and music educators, Gregory Blankenbehler enjoyed singing before he could talk and began formal piano and violin lessons at four. As a child, he participated in countless musical theater, choir, band, orchestra and drama experiences, while always holding a special love for solo singing. Pursuing that love, Gregory earned a bachelor's and master's degree in vocal performance and completed several opera training programs. Performance opportunities have taken him to England, France and Italy; to San Jose and San Francisco to perform lead opera roles, and to Salt Lake City to solo with the Mormon Tabernacle Choir.

Gregory discovered his joy and talent for teaching others during his undergraduate studies when he began teaching voice, as well as tutoring students in music theory and ear-training. This interest led him to undergo a major comparative study of voice training and performance techniques for his master's education. Since then, Gregory has balanced his performing career with a full studio of voice and piano students of all ages and abilities. In his desire to provide individualized instruction to all of his music students, Gregory keenly noticed the special challenges involved in teaching voice to very young children. Not finding any age-appropriate voice method available, he has created this book as the beginning of an early-age curriculum to bring children to enjoy the pleasures and benefits of music as he did.

Gregory Blankenbehler currently resides in San Jose, California with his wife Erica, a talented artist and chiropractor.

[1] G. Schlaug, L. Jancke, Y. Huang and H. Steinmetz, "In vivo morphometry of interhem ispheric assymetry and connectivity in musicians," Proceedings of the 3rd international conference for music perception and cognition (Liege, Belgium, 1994) pp. 417-418.

[2] Amy Graziano, Matthew Peterson and Gordon Shaw, "Enhanced learning of proportional math through music training and spatial-temporal training," *Neurological Research* 21 (March 1999).

[3] *College-Bound Seniors National Report: Profile of SAT Program Test Takers*. The College Entrance Examination Board, Princeton, NJ, 2001.

[4] Rauscher, Shaw, Levine, Ky and Wright, "Music and Spatial Task Performance: A Causal Relationship," University of California, Irvine, 1994.

[5] Lewis Thomas, "The Case for Music in the Schools," *Phi Delta Kappan* (February 1994).

[6] "The Case for Sequential Music Education in the Core Curriculum of the Public Schools," The Center for the Arts in the Basic Curriculum, New York, 1989.

[7] Shinichi Suzuki, *Nurtured by Love*, Second Ed., Athens OH: Senzay Publications, 1983, pp. 79, 15.

Table of Contents

UNIT I: Singing Fundamentals

Stretches are very important for the little singer. They promote proper posture and alignment, prime the trunk muscles for use and remind the singer that singing is done with the whole body and not just the throat. The first three stretches should be repeated at the beginning of every lesson and practice session. The last exercise is good for little singers who are still sleepy, or generally uncoordinated. It should be tried a few times and subsequently used as needed.

Stretches

Reach for a Star Stretch: Stand on your tippy-toes and reach one hand high up to the sky. Now do the same with the other hand. Feel the stretch in your arms, stomach, legs and other places.

Hula-hoop Stretch: With your hands on your waist, bend your hips around in a circle; one way and then the other. Feel the stretch in your stomach, low back and upper legs.

Ragdoll Stretch: Bend over and reach for your toes. Feel the stretch in your legs and low back. Now roll back up on your spine from the bottom to the top. First your stomach straightens, then your chest, then your shoulders and last of all your neck then head.

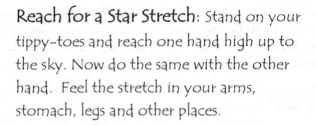

Body-Mind Connection Exercise:

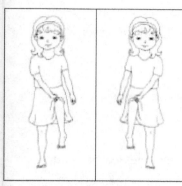

1. Touch your right hand to your left knee. Now touch your left hand to your right knee. Return to normal. Repeat each side 1 more time.

2. In front of your body, touch your left foot to your right hand. Now, your right foot to your left hand. Repeat 1 time.

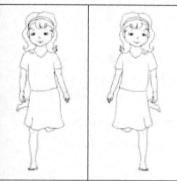

3. Behind your body, touch your left foot to your right hand. Now, your right foot to your left hand. Repeat 1 time.

4. Touch your left knee to your left hand. Now do the right side. Repeat 1 time.

Keep cycling through steps 1-4, going faster each time, until the heart is pumping and the mind is focused.

Like a machine, in order for the body to work properly to sing well, it must be put together right. It should be straight, relaxed and poised to work as it was designed. This exercise and "posture check" should also be performed at the beginning of every lesson and practice session.

Posture

Good Morning Sunshine Exercise: Stand and raise your hands up to the sky. Turn them so your palms face inward, toward each other. Now, while keeping your arms straight, lower your arms sideways down your body in a circle until they reach your legs. Relax your shoulders but keep your chest in this raised position. This is how your body should be for singing.

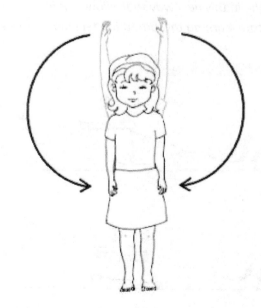

Posture Check:

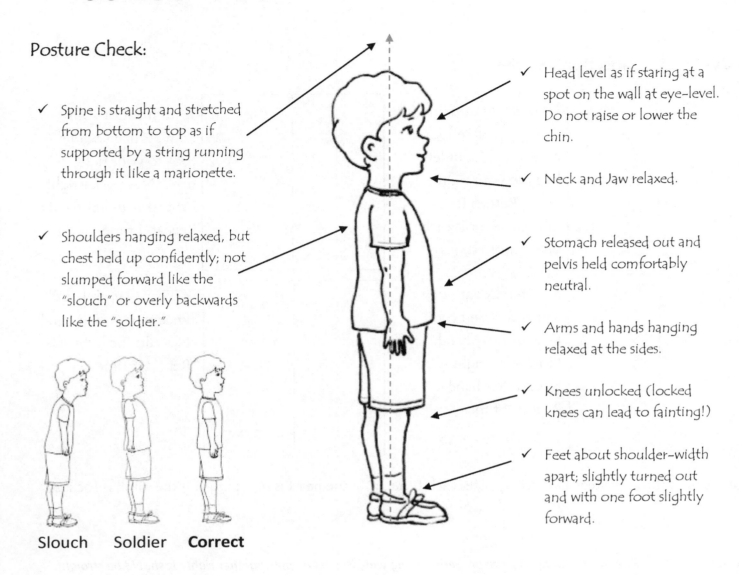

- ✓ Spine is straight and stretched from bottom to top as if supported by a string running through it like a marionette.

- ✓ Shoulders hanging relaxed, but chest held up confidently; not slumped forward like the "slouch" or overly backwards like the "soldier."

- ✓ Head level as if staring at a spot on the wall at eye-level. Do not raise or lower the chin.

- ✓ Neck and Jaw relaxed.

- ✓ Stomach released out and pelvis held comfortably neutral.

- ✓ Arms and hands hanging relaxed at the sides.

- ✓ Knees unlocked (locked knees can lead to fainting!)

- ✓ Feet about shoulder-width apart; slightly turned out and with one foot slightly forward.

Slouch   Soldier   **Correct**

Ultimately, singing is a very refined kind of breathing. To sing well, it is very important that the little singer learn how to breathe in this new way that allows them to sing with longer and more beautiful tones than they would otherwise. To facilitate learning this breathing technique, these next exercises should be reviewed every lesson and practice session.

Breathing

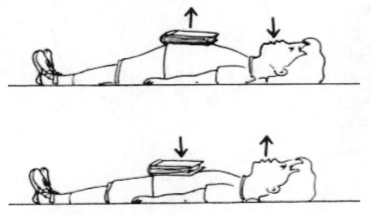

Belly Breathing Exercise: Lay face up on the floor and place a book of comfortable weight on your stomach. Breathe low into your stomach and make the book rise with the air. (The chest may also rise but do not move the shoulders!) Slowly let the air escape through your mouth; the book will slowly lower. Repeat this several times to build the muscles for breathing in and train the breath to go into the stomach and not the shoulders.

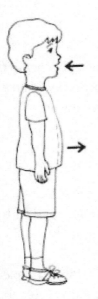

Inhaling and Suspending Exercise: Standing with good posture, take a deep breath in by opening your mouth, throat and nasal passages wide and filling your stomach from the bottom up. Keep good posture throughout and do not let the shoulders or upper chest rise! Hold (suspend) the air in this position for several seconds without closing your throat. A fly should be able to fly down into your lungs if it tried. Practice this a few times.

Exhaling Exercise: Breath in correctly. Then close your teeth and begin to hiss, gently but steadily pushing the air up out of your stomach with your lower abdominal (stomach) muscles. The chest and shoulders should hold their position until the end—do not ever let the chest collapse to squeeze air out of there! (Try this exercise again buzzing the lips, rolling the tongue, making a "zzzzz" sound and humming.)

1-2-3-4 Breathing Exercise: This exercise practices the 4 steps of the breath cycle that singers should go through every time they sing. The teacher will show which step you are on by holding up that number of fingers.

1. **Inhalation.** Breathe in correctly (following the inhaling exercise).
2. **Suspension.** Hold the position keeping the throat and lungs open. (A fly should be able to fly down your throat into your lungs.) Think about what it sounds and feels like to start singing.
3. **Exhalation.** Hiss out, hum or sing (following the exhaling or siren exercises).
4. **Rest.** Stop singing and gently let out the remaining air out of the belly, if any. Still keep good posture and do not collapse or attempt to squeeze air out of the chest or shoulders.

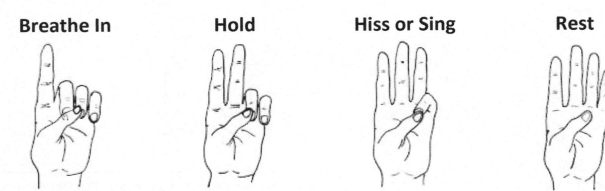

Breathe In   **Hold**   **Hiss or Sing**   **Rest**

Teacher Note: Do Step 1 for about 5 seconds, Step 2 for about 5 seconds, Step 3 for about 10 seconds and Step 4 for about 3 seconds. Repeat the cycle several times, trying to increase the lengths of the steps.

In order to prevent unhealthy straining, it is important to make the little singer comfortable with singing in either of his or her two voices. It is also important that they learn the abstract concepts of pitch level. These concepts and exercises (or advanced variations of them presented in later units) should be reviewed every lesson and practice session.

The Low and High Voice

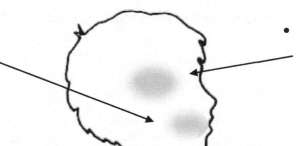

- **The low voice** vibrates in the mouth (find the area by singing "hum").

  It is the normal talking voice, but gets tight and strained when used too high

- **The high voice** vibrates above in the head (find the area by singing "hung").

  It is a comfortable, relaxed way to sing high notes, but gets too weak and breathy when used too low.

Voices Levels Exercise: Humming (closed lips but open jaw!) or on "ah," the student alternates between low and high voice, mimicking the teacher and following the indication of the teacher's hand. Next, add a "middle" position to the alternation. (Advanced students can do short 3 or 5 note slides or scales to exercise and develop the two voices.)

Siren Exercise: Humming or on "ah," slide up from your lowest pitch, through both voices hitting every pitch, to your highest pitch. The voice should be "lifted" up and over to the high voice rather than "punched" through. Then take a breath and repeat this from your highest to lowest pitch. (Try doing up and down in one breath. Try down and up. Advanced students try different vowels, slower and with no gaps in the slide.)

Teacher Note: *The new singer typically has a strong low voice and a weak, breathy high voice with difficulty transitioning in between. With patient practice and experience, the upper voice will strengthen and transition will become easier. New little singers also typically have some trouble matching many of the middle pitches. With patient voice level, siren, scale and interval work, this difficulty will also soon disappear.*

UNIT II: The Scale

Fundamental to learning to sing is mastering the steps of the scale. The following exercises should be done every lesson to ensure accuracy of pitch and memorization of the solfegge syllables. With this background, the little singer will be in the best position to learn effective sight-singing, as well as good vocal technique. (In addition to the songs provided, the following may be used for studying the scale: "I'm a Little Teapot," "Joy to the World" and "Do-re-mi.")

Up the Scale:

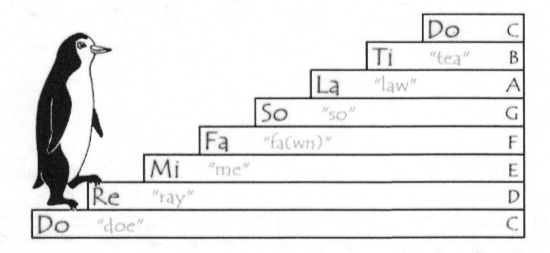

Down the Scale:

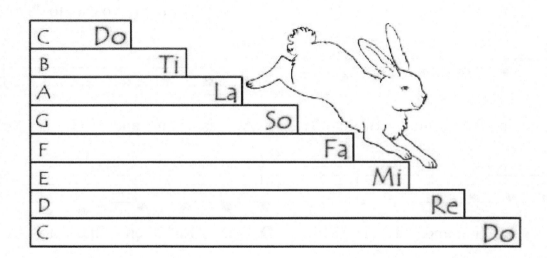

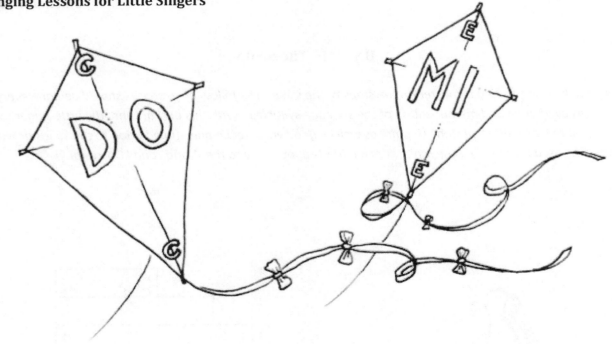

"C is Do and D is Re"

By G. Blankenbehler

C is "Do" and   D is "Re",   E is "Mi" and   F is "Fa",

G is "So" and   A is "La",   B is "Ti" then   back to "Do".

C   is "Do" and   B is "Ti",   A   is "La" and   G is "So",

F   is "Fa and   E   is "Mi",   D   is "Re" then   back to C.

"Merrily We Roll Along"

Traditional Folk Song

Mer - ri - ly we roll a - long,   Roll a - long,   Roll a - long.

Mer - ri - ly we roll a - long,   O'er the deep blue sea.

"Little Things"

Traditional French Melody, Words by Julia A. Fletcher

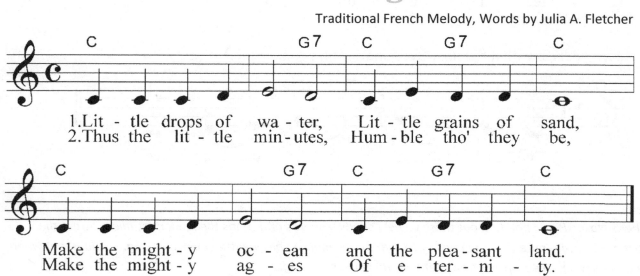

1. Lit - tle drops of wa - ter,   Lit - tle grains of sand,
2. Thus the lit - tle min - utes, Hum - ble tho' they be,

Make the might - y   oc - ean and the plea - sant land.
Make the might - y   ag - es Of e - ter - ni - ty.

Technique: Primary Vowels

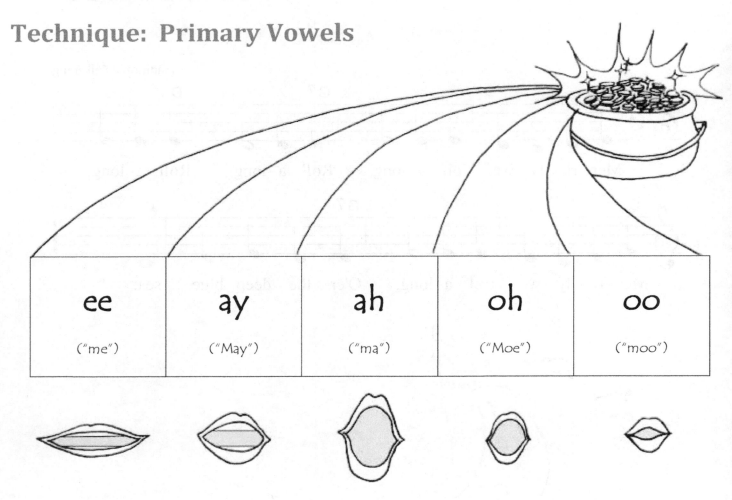

ee	ay	ah	oh	oo
("me")	("May")	("ma")	("Moe")	("moo")

Exercise 1: (Repeat with different beginning consonants)

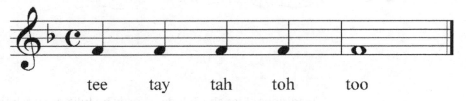

tee   tay   tah   toh   too

Exercise 2: (Repeat with different vowels and starting consonants)

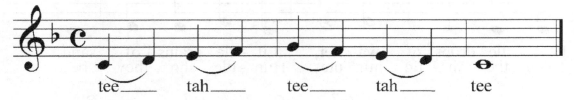

tee____   tah____   tee____   tah____   tee

Teacher's Note: *Begin pointing out these vowel sounds in words and songs the student studies. Stress the importance of using pure vowel sounds, rather than the impure ones we use when speaking. Explain that when singing, we sometimes say things differently than when speaking.*

UNIT III: Steps and Seconds

Often, a little singer will initially have difficulty matching each and every step of the scale.   However, when presented with the intervals individually, starting with the step and gradually moving to the larger ones, over time they learn to sing them without difficulty. (Additional songs that can be used with this unit are: "Frère Jaques," "Hot Cross Buns," "London Bridge," "Mary Had a Little Lamb," "Row, Row, Row Your Boat" and "Yankee Doodle.")

Stepping Upwards:

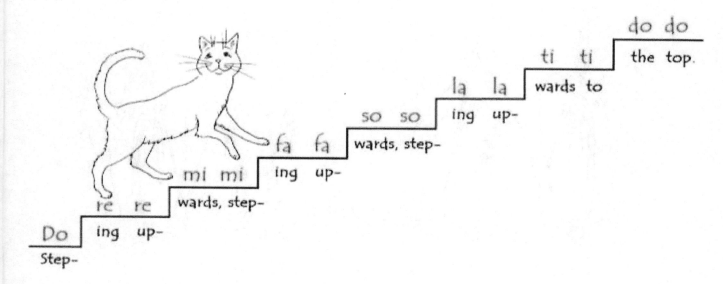

Stepping Downwards:

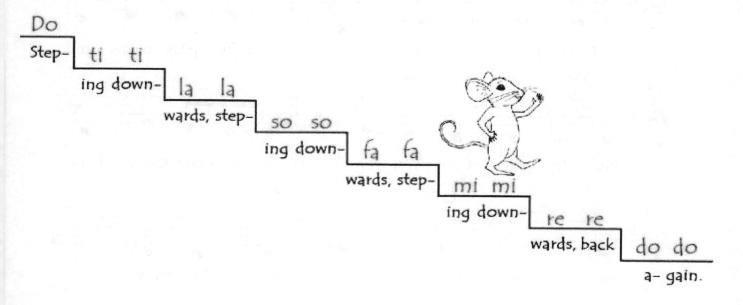

Just a Second...

Just   a   sec - ond,   just   a   sec - ond...____
(Do - Re   Do - Re   Do - Re   Do - Re)____

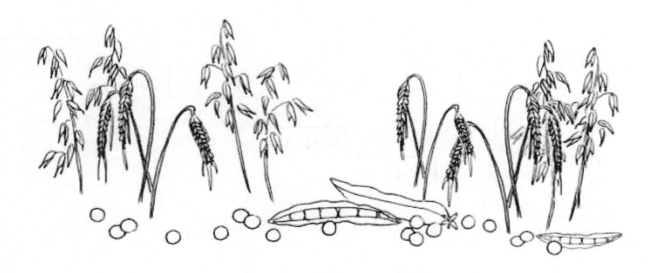

"Oats, Peas, Beans and Barley Grow"

Traditional Nursery Rhyme

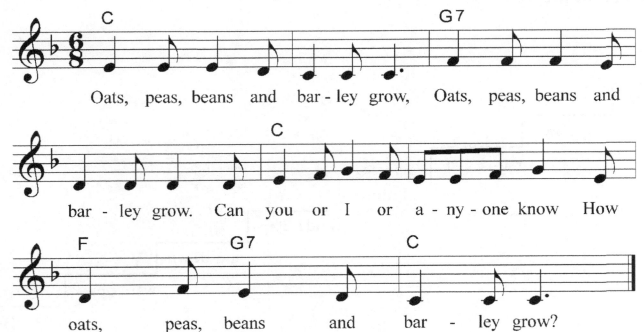

Oats, peas, beans and bar - ley grow,   Oats, peas, beans and

bar - ley grow.   Can you or I or a - ny - one know How

oats,   peas, beans   and   bar - ley grow?

"Down by the Station"

American Folk Song

Down   by   the   sta - tion   ear - ly   in   the   morn - ing,

See   the   lit - tle   puf - fer   bel - lies   all   in   a   row.

See   the   en - gin - eer   man   pull   the   great   big   throt - tle

Choo! - Choo!   Toot!   Toot!   Off   they   go.

Technique: Tongue, Mouth and Throat Posture

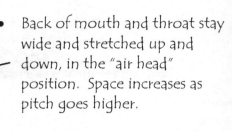

- Face relaxed, feels like it's just hanging there.

- Jaw stays open: 2 fingers high for "ah" and "oh," a little less for others.

- Tip of tongue stays at base of bottom teeth **for all vowels**.

- Back of mouth and throat stay wide and stretched up and down, in the "air head" position. Space increases as pitch goes higher.

- Buzz during low voice is felt in "cool spot" and above for higher notes.

The Tongue Test Exercise: Practice saying the 5 different vowels individually, all the time keeping the tip of the tongue at the inner base of the lower front teeth and the front of the tongue wide and flat or slightly furrowed. Also, look for the correct amount of jaw opening. Then, practice them in pairs, transitioning smoothly and quickly from the first to the second vowel.

Creating the "Air Head": Try the following to see what it feels like to open the throat and back of mouth: 1) Yawn. (Without pulling the tongue back, this is the correct position.) 2) Breathe deeply through the nose like you're smelling something wonderful. 3) Imagine you are singing with a boiled egg between and behind your upper molars. Imagine your head is hollow and the sound echoes in the open space. Practice increasing this expansion with sirens: the higher the pitch, the more opening needed.

Finding the "Cool Spot": Breathe in the mouth deeply and quickly. The area in between and behind the upper molars will feel cool from the rushing air. Do the same but through the nose. The "cool spot" lies between the cool areas you felt in the roof of the mouth and the nose.

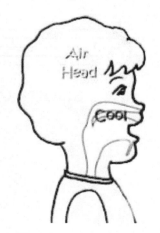

Singing in the "Cool Spot": Direct the air coming up through the throat along the back wall of the mouth and into the "cool spot" causing it to buzz.

Teacher's Note: Use Primary Vowel exercises for the Tongue Test Exercise, and any simple exercises for the "Cool Spot" exercises. Let proper tone focus and resonance be your guide in directing the student.

UNIT IV: Skips and Thirds

Once the little singer has gained some proficiency in the pitches and syllables of the scale, they can begin working on larger intervals. Both the words and solfegge syllables should be practiced in each exercise. They should also be transposed up and down. Technical skills should be addressed as they are introduced.   (Additional songs for working on thirds include "Camptown Races," "The Mulberry Bush," "Mairzy Doats" and "On Top of Old Smokey.")

Thirds are Skips:

Thirds are   skips and   skips are   thirds.
(Do - Mi   Do - Mi   Do - Mi   Do)

Singing's Fun!

Sing - ing,   sing - ing's   fun!
(Do - Mi   So - Mi   Do)

Bumble Bee Exercise:

Bum-ble bee___ bum-ble bee___ bum-ble bee___ bum-ble bee.

Bum-ble bee___ bum-ble bee___ bum-ble bee___ bum-ble bee.

Arpeggio Exercise:

I'd like to fly like a plane.
(Do - Mi - So   Do - So - Mi   Do.)

"My Skipping Song"

By G. Blankenbehler

Skip - ping, skip - ping all day long, As I

sing my skip-ping song. Skip - ping, skip - ping all day

through; I love skip - ping, Don't you?

"Lightly Row"

American Folk Song

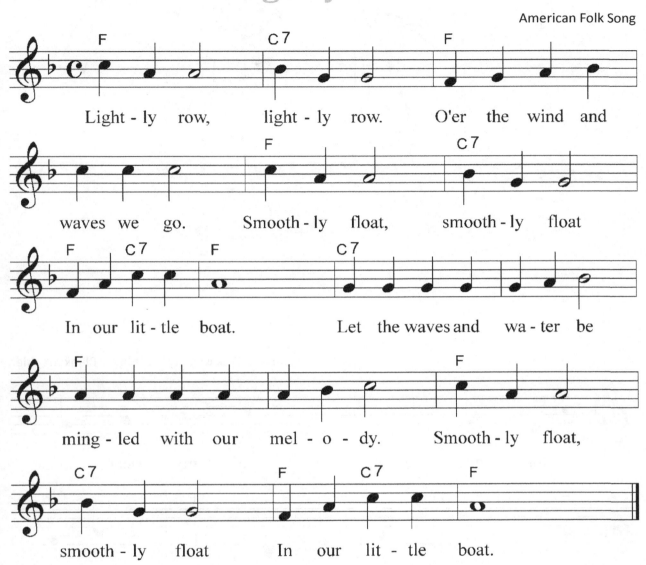

Light - ly row,   light - ly row.   O'er the wind and waves we go.   Smooth - ly float,   smooth - ly float   In our lit - tle boat.   Let the waves and wa - ter be ming - led with our mel - o - dy.   Smooth - ly float,   smooth - ly float   In our lit - tle boat.

"Gone to Play!"

German Folk Melody, Text by G. Blankenbehler

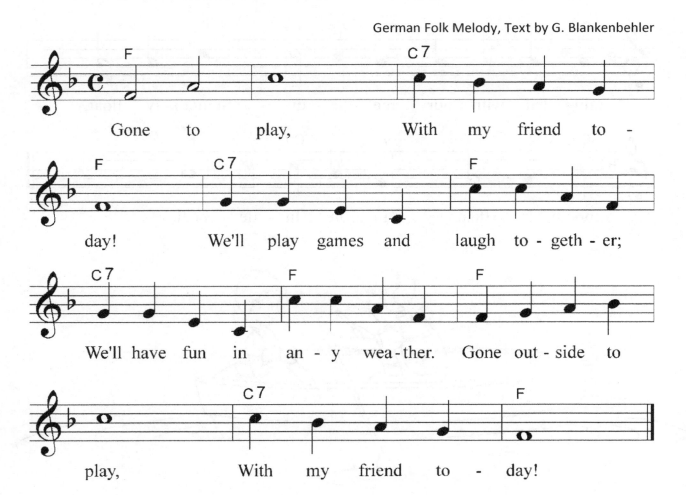

Gone   to   play,   With   my   friend   to -

day!   We'll   play   games   and   laugh   to - geth - er;

We'll   have   fun   in   an - y   wea - ther.   Gone out - side   to

play,   With   my   friend   to -   day!

Technique: Diphthongs

1ˢᵗ Vowel Very Long,   2ⁿᵈ Vowel Very Short!

A = <u>ay</u> + ee

I = <u>ah</u> + ee

O = <u>oh</u> + oo

ow = <u>ah</u> + oo

oy = <u>oh</u> + ee

R = <u>ah</u> + ruh

Diphthong Exercise: (Repeat with all diphthongs)

AH_____ (ee)

My! Say! No! Now! Boy! Car! Exercise: (Repeat with each word)

My!_____ (ee)

Teacher's Note: It is usually a surprise to little singers that letters they were taught as vowels in school are actually made up of two other vowels. Have the student sound these diphthongs out slowly, stressing the importance of pure vowels (without any "corruption" of the first vowel by the second), a quick and smooth transition from the first to second vowel, and the elongated nature of the first vowel with the extremely minimal nature of the second. The student must also learn to refrain from holding the "American 'R'" and instead minimize its length and nasal tone. Alternate words can of course be substituted in the second exercise.

UNIT V: Fourths

With the introduction of the interval of the fourth, the little singer should continue to review certain of the exercises of past chapters, as well as continuing work on vowel precision, resonance placement and registration.   (Additional "fourths" songs: "The Farmer in the Dell," "Down in the Valley," "Hokey Pokey" and "I've Been Working on the Railroad.")

Singing 4 Steps:

How Lovely!:

"Fourths are Fun!"

By G. Blankenbehler (With apologies to W. A. Mozart)

Fourths are   fun   to   sing   if   you know   how.

Skip   two   keys, you've   done it! Take   a   bow!

"Aura Lee"

Words by W. W. Fosdick, Music by George R. Poulton

1.As   the   black - bird   in   the   spring,   'neath   the   wil - low
2.When   the   mis - tle - toe   was   green,   midst   the   win - ter's

tree   Sat   and   piped,   I   heard   him   sing,   sing   of   Au - ra
snows,   Sun - shine   in   thy   face   was   seen,   kiss - ing   lips   of

Lee.   Au - ra   Lee,   Au - ra   Lee,   maid   with   gold - en   hair.
rose.   Au - ra   Lee,   Au - ra   Lee,   take   my   gold - en   ring,

Sun - shine   came   a - long   with   thee,   and   swal - lows   in   the   air.
Love   and   light   re - turn   with   thee,   and   swal - lows   with   the   spring.

"My Grandfather's Clock"

By Henry Clay Work

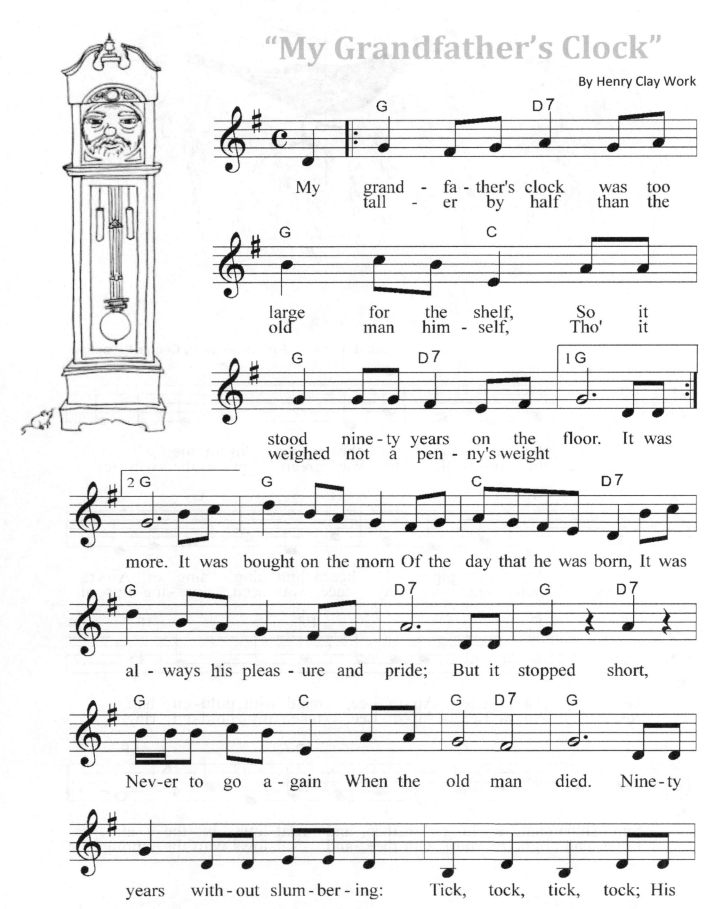

My   grand - fa - ther's clock   was   too
tall - er   by   half   than   the

large   for   the   shelf,   So   it
old   man   him - self,   Tho'   it

stood   nine - ty years   on   the   floor.   It was
weighed   not   a   pen - ny's weight

more.   It was   bought on the morn Of the   day that he was born, It was

al - ways his pleas - ure   and   pride;   But it   stopped   short,

Nev - er to go   a - gain   When the   old   man   died.   Nine - ty

years   with - out slum - ber - ing: Tick,   tock,   tick,   tock; His

life-sec-onds num-ber-ing: Tick, tock, tick, tock; It stopped short,

Ne-ver to go a - gain When the old man died.

"I'm the Best at Being Me"

By G. Blankenbehler

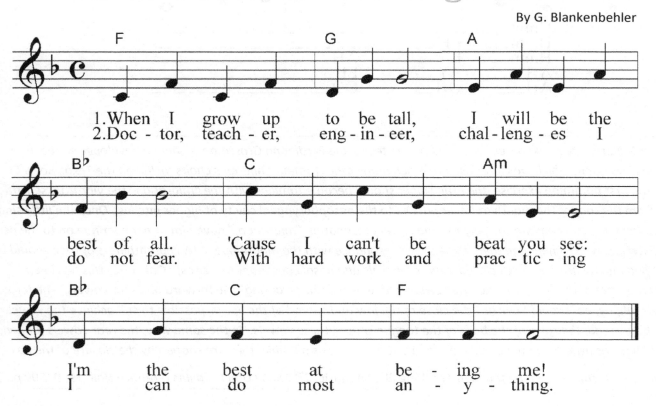

1. When I grow up to be tall, I will be the
2. Doc - tor, teach - er, eng - in - eer, chal - leng - es I

best of all. 'Cause I can't be beat you see:
do not fear. With hard work and prac - tic - ing

I'm the best at be - ing me!
I can do most an - y - thing.

Technique: Tone Building

- "Air Head" space made by yawning (Don't pull back the tongue!) and empty head feeling.

- "Cool Spot" found by breathing in and feeling the cool place made by the rushing air in the roof of the mouth.

How to Hum: From the "ee" vowel position, gently close the lips but still keep the teeth more than a finger's width apart. Open up the "air head" space and try to fill as much of your head with sound as possible. The "buzz" should be felt in the lower "cool spot" area, as well as the teeth, lips, and nose area. As the pitch rises, the buzz will move from the mouth into the upper "cool spot" and the "air head" space (changing from "hmmm" to "hung"). Expanding the "air head" space for high notes will make them much easier to sing well.

Voice Builder Exercises:

Hmm
Hmm____ EE
Hmm____ EE____ AH
AH____ AY____ EE
AH____ OH____ OO

Teacher's Note: These exercises are based on the technique Ferdinand Grossman of Vienna developed to teach the Vienna Boys Choir, which was later used to teach many other famous children's choirs including the Texas Boy's Choir. * With the first humming exercise, the little singer should become familiar with the "migration" the vibratory sensations take from the roof of the mouth at lower pitches to the nasopharyngeal cavity at higher pitches. Once the little singer remembers and can consistently perform the correct resonating "migration," have him or her continue on to the next two exercises which challenge them to keep this resonance with the mouth open. (Any breathiness of tone should be identified and focused out with closed forward vowels and nasal consonant exercises). Only after this has been mastered, should the final two exercises be started, which entail "tracking" the forward and rear vowels. The forward vowels (ah, ay, ee) should have as little close of the jaw and spread of the lips as possible to still achieve the vowel sounds. Instead, the raise of the back of the tongue shapes these vowels. In the same way, the rear vowels (ah, oh, oo) should have as little movement inside the mouth and throat as possible; they are shaped by the closure of the lips.

* The entire technique can be found in Teaching Choral Music, *2ⁿᵈ Ed. by Don L. Collins (Prentice Hall, 1999, 509 pp.)*

UNIT VI: Fifths

As the interval jumps get bigger, it becomes increasingly important for the little singer to be able to instantaneously and effectively shift between registers and resonance positions. Exercises and songs should be attempted slowly until accuracy of interval movement is mastered. (Additional fifths songs: "Twinkle Twinkle Little Star"/"ABC Song"/"Baa Baa Black Sheep" and "If You're Happy and You Know It.")

Oh–wee –oh!:

I Love to Sing:

"I Can Sing a Perfect Fifth"

By G. Blankenbehler

"Lavender's Blue"

English Folk Song

Lav - en - der's blue, dil - ly dil - ly,
Who told you so, dil - ly dil - ly,

Lav - en - der's green, When I am
Who told you so? 'Twas my own

King, dil - ly dil - ly, You shall be Queen.
heart, dil - ly dil - ly, That told me so.

"Oh Ice Cream Man!"

By G. Blankenbehler (With apologies to all parents)

1.Oh   ice   cream   man,   ice   cream   man,   please   stop   for   me!   I
2.The   straw - ber - ry   freeze - ie's   the   best   that I   see, Or_a

hear   your   bells   ring - ing   and   just   want   to   see,   The
cho - co - late   sand - wich   with   ice   cream   be - tween.   Oh

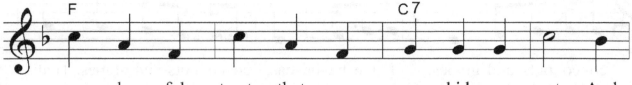

won - der - ful   treats   that   a   young   kid   can   get   And
ice   cream   man,   ice   cream   man,   please   stop   for   me!   My

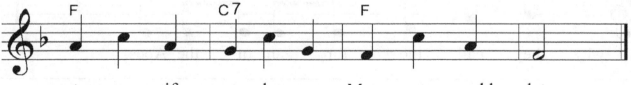

eat   some   if   on - ly   my   Mom - my   would   let.
mom   gave   me   mon - ey   and   I   am   hun - gry!

Technique: Secondary Vowels

Secondary Vowels Exercise: (Repeat for all vowel pairs, changing initial consonants)

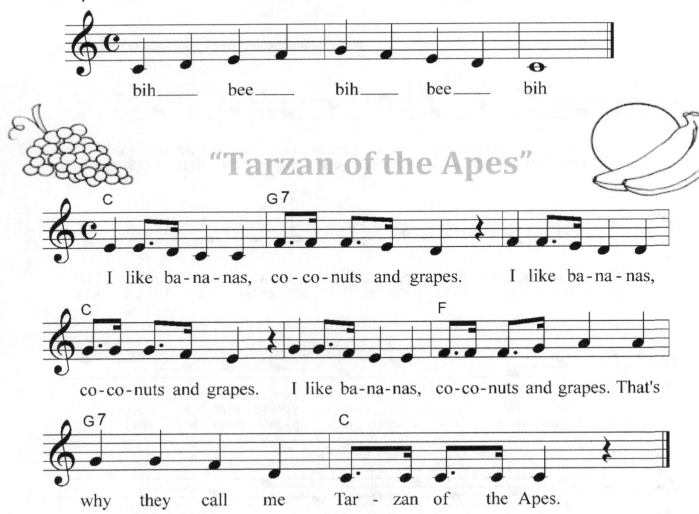

Repeat the song for each vowel, changing every vowel in the phrase "I like bananas, coconuts and grapes" to the vowel you've chosen. (Example: "ee leek bee-nee-nees, kee-kee-neets eend greeps.")

UNIT VII: Sixths

In addition to instantaneous, accurate interval jumps, the little singer should be singing with accurate diction and improved tone quality. The teacher may also wish to begin introducing expression and interpretation into the songs and exercises. (Additional sixths songs: "My Bonnie Lies Over the Ocean," "Billy Boy" and "Old MacDonald Had a Farm.")

Good Morning!

Good morn-ing, good morn-ing, good morn - ing!
(Do - La - Fa Do - La - Fa Do - La - Fa)

Sing High, Sing Low:

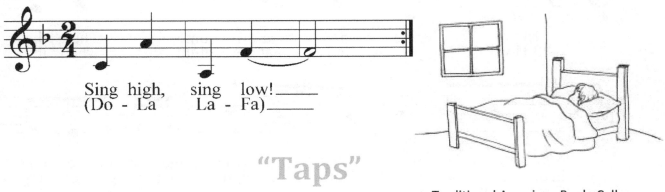

Sing high, sing low!_____
(Do - La La - Fa)_____

"Taps"

Traditional American Bugle Call

1. Day is done, gone the sun, From the
2. Go to sleep, peace-ful sleep. May the

hills, from the lake, From the skies. All is
sold - ier or sail - or God keep, On the

well, Safe - ly rest, God is nigh.
land or the deep, Safe in sleep.

"Home on the Range"

Cowboy Folk Song

1.Oh give me a home, where the buf-fa-lo roam, Where the deer and the an-te-lope play;_____ Where sel-dom is heard a dis-cour-ag-ing word, And the skys are not cloud-y all day._____

2.How of-ten at night when the heav-ens are bright With the lights from the glit-ter-ing stars,_____ Have I stood there a-mazed and asked as I gazed If their glo-ry ex-ceeds that of ours_____

Home, home on the range, Where the deer and the an-te-lope

play;   Where sel - dom is heard   a dis -

cour - ag - ing word,   And the skys are not cloud - y all day.

"The Holly and the Ivy"

Traditional English Carol

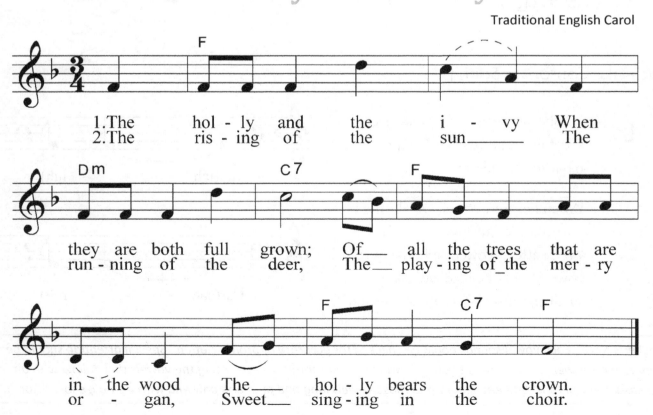

1.The   hol - ly   and   the   i - vy   When
2.The   ris - ing   of   the   sun_____   The

they are both   full   grown;   Of__ all the trees   that are
run - ning of   the   deer,   The__ play - ing of_the   mer - ry

in   the wood   The____ hol - ly bears   the   crown.
or - gan,   Sweet____ sing - ing in   the   choir.

Technique: Consonants

Simple Consonant Sounds:

B D F G H K M N P S T V W Z

Compound Consonant Sounds:

Qu (= kw)   X (= ks)   Sh   Th (voiced & unvoiced)

Short "EE" Consonant Sounds:

Y (=ee + <u>uh</u>)   J   Ch

Vowel-Like Consonant Sounds:

L   "L" should always be pronounced short in singing as "luh" and not nasalized as "all."

Tall(tah - - - luh)

R   When before a vowel, "R" should be pronounced quickly.
When after a vowel, only the pure vowel should be held with only a very small and un-nasal "ruh" at the end.

Car(cah - - - ruh)

Teacher's Note: Each vowel sound should be checked for accuracy of pronunciation. Special attention should be given to the "Vowel-Like Consonant Sounds," which are notorious for corrupting the vowels they follow with an unpleasant, nasal tone. Student should sing those vowels long and pure and only end with a small, short "l" or "r."

UNIT VIII: Sevenths and Octaves

With sevenths being perhaps the hardest interval and octaves the easiest, they are presented together to facilitate learning. Again, interpretation and acting may be addressed on these songs. (Additional seventh and octave songs: "Somewhere over the Rainbow," "Happy Birthday to You" and "Take Me Out to the Ballgame")

Sing a Seventh:

Sing   a   sev - enth._____
(Do - Do   Ti - Do)_____

Singing a Jazzy Chord:

Sing - ing   a   jaz - zy   chord.
(Do - Mi - So - Ti So - Mi - Do)

I Love All My Friends:

I   love   all   my   friends.
(So   Fa - Mi - Re - Do)

"I Wish on a Star"

By G. Blankenbehler

1.I wish on a star that shines far and bright; A
2.And just like my star, that al - ways shines true, I

dream that I hope for,___ I ask on this night. I
will show my spec - ial light in all that I do. Each

wish for a life___ of beau - ty and peace, A
star is so dif - ferent u - nique as you and me, And

life___ of suc - cess - es of joy___ with - out cease.
if we work to - geth - er, we'll shine for all to see!

I be - lieve that great things will come, As sure as the

o-ceans, as sure as the sun. And I   be - lieve the stars want me to suc-

ceed; They shine there to in - spire me to be all I can be.

"Old Folks at Home"

By Stephen Foster

'Way down up - on the   Swa - nee Riv - er,   Far, far a - way;
All   up and down the whole cre - a - tion, Sad - ly I roam;

There's where my heart is turn - ing e - ver, There's where the old folks
Still   long - ing for the old plant - a - tion, And   for the old folks at

stay.   All the world is sad and drear - y, Ev - 'ry - where I roam;
home.

Oh! la - dies, how my heart grows wear - y, Far from the old folks at home.

Technique: Legato Singing

SmoooooooothlyyyyyyyyyyIIIIIIIIIIICooooooonneeeeeeect!!!

Legato – Single Note:

1. AhhhhhhhEhhhhhhhhEeeeeeeeeeOhhhhhhhhOoooooooo
2. MahhhhhhhMehhhhhhhhMeeeeeeeeeMohhhhhhMooooooo

Legato – Scale:

1. AhhhhhhhhhEhhhhhhhhhEeeeeeeeeeeOhhhhhhhhhOoooooooo
2. MahhhhhhhhhMehhhhhhhhhMeeeeeeeeeMohhhhhhhhhMoooooooo

Legato – Words:

SmoooooothleeeeeeeAhhhh(ee)CawwwwwNehhhhctEeeeeechWuhhhhhhhh(r)d
(Smooth - ly   I   con - nect   each   word;

Ahhhhh(ee)CaaaaaaaanSeeeeeeengLuhhhhhhhhgahhhhhhtohhhhhhhTooooooooooooo
I   can   sing   le - ga - to   too!)

Teacher's Note: Students should first work on transitioning quickly and smoothly between vowels on a held note while maintaining even tone and support. Once mastered, consonants should be added between the vowels to be executed with the same smoothness and evenness (no breaks or pops). These goals should then be attempted on the scale, and finally with words. Earlier songs and exercises should also be reviewed focusing on legato production.

UNIT IX: Half-Steps

While it may be difficult for the little singers who have not studied other music instruments to understand the difference between accidentals, they should have little trouble with the half-step interval or minor scale. (Additional half-step songs: "When Johnny Comes Marching Home Again," "What Child is This," "When You Wish Upon a Star," "Part of Your World" and many other Disney Songs.)

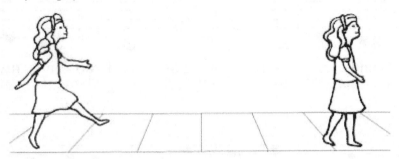

Take a Whole-Step, Take a Half-Step:

Take a whole step, Take a half-step, It's a small-er step.

Sing a Half-Step, Sing a Whole Step:

Sing a half-step, Sing a whole-step, Sing a half-step now.

Sing a Minor Scale:

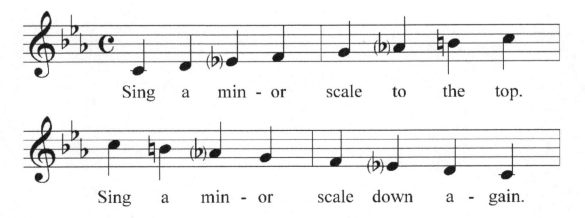

Sing a min - or scale to the top.

Sing a min - or scale down a - gain.

"If I Had a Big Robot"

By G. Blankenbehler

1.If   I   had   a   big ro - bot   that   would   do   all   my   wish-es;
2.And, of course, he'd   go   to school with   me   when   I   would   need him.

I   would   ne - ver   have   to   sweep   the   floor   or   do   the   dish - es.
He   could   help me   with   my   school work   or   play   on   my   team in gym.

There would   be   no   more of "Clean your   room!" or "Mow the   lawn to-day!"
And   if   bul-lies   tried   to   pick   on   me   or   tried   to   block my way.

I   would   simp-ly   tell   my   ro-bot   and   he   would   say,   "Right a-way!"
I   would   simp-ly   tell   my   ro-bot   and   he   would   say,   "Right a-way!"

"Halloween"

By G. Blankenbehler

1. When Oct - o - ber comes a - round it casts a ma - gic
2. Au - tumn wears her cost - ume too, all dressed in red and

spell.   Glow - ing fac - es greet you from a jack - o - lant - ern
gold;   Bright be - neath the har - vest moon her col - ored leaves un -

shell.   Soon the ghosts and witch - es at your
fold.   Sip - ping ap - ple ci - der, we take

door - step will be seen.   Com - ing to say
in this charm - ing scene.   No - thing could be

"Trick or treat!" for this is Hal - low - een!
bet - ter than a Hap - py Hal - low - een!

"Be Kind to Your Web-Footed Friends"

Attr. to Mitch Miller (with apologies to John Philip Sousa)

Be kind to your web-foot-ed friends,_____ For a

duck may be some-bod-y's moth - er._____ Be

kind to your friends in the swamp,_____ Where it's

ve-ry, ve-ry, ve-ry, ve-ry damp. (Two! Three!) You

may think that this is the end._____ Well it is.

Technique: Performance Skills

Performance experience is an important part of the little singer's development into a musician. While at first it can be scary, with proper preparation and techniques performing should be a very rewarding experience.

Practice and Prepare: First, learn to sing your song memorized without any mistakes. Then, practice performing it in front of your parents, friends and even a mirror to become more comfortable singing in front of people. On the day of your performance, arrive early and bring your music with you.

Play Pretend: Good performers don't just sing their songs, they act them out too. Acting is really no more than just playing pretend: Pretend that you are the character in the song you are singing and do what you think they would do. Your teacher will help you choose appropriate actions and expressions for acting out your song.

Don't worry. Have fun! First performances can sometimes be scary, but there is really nothing to be afraid of. Your teacher will be there to help if anything goes wrong, and your parents and friends watching will cheer you on and clap for you no matter what happens. No performance is ever perfect so just do your best and enjoy sharing with others the songs you have learned!

Teacher's Note: Every little singer comes with a different level of comfort in front of others. For some, being pushed too soon into performing can have lasting negative effects. If a little singer seems particularly troubled about performing in front of others, the teacher and parents should pay close attention to ascertain whether the child is ready or whether their first performance should be postponed until a later recital.

Graduation Song

Words by G. Blankenbehler, Traditional Irish Folk Song "The Flight of the Earls"

1. My sing-ing les-sons___ have been fun, I've
2. I love to sing___ and___ to per-form, And

learned so ma-ny___ things; And now this sing-ing___
oth-ers like___ it___ too; My tal-ent's grow-ing___

book is done, I'm off to great-er___ things. There's
ev-'ry day, And there's so much___ to___ do. My

so much more that I can learn, So ma-ny songs to
fam-i-ly, friends help me to know I real-ly can suc-

sing; If I will pract - ice___ pat - ient-ly, I
ceed; If I will pract - ice___ pat - ient-ly, I

can do an - y___ thing!
will have all___ I___ need.

This Certificate Confirms that

has completed

Singing Lessons for Little Singers

and is ready for further singing adventures!

Teacher _____

Date _____

Made in the USA
Coppell, TX
09 October 2023

22601764R00031